1949

Yours lovingly in Our Lady,

Sister M. Theresa, S.L.

This book may be ke

A fine will be c

DE 14 '67

JA 4 '68

GIVE JOAN A SWORD

THE MACMILLAN COMPANY
NEW YORK · BOSTON · CHICAGO
DALLAS · ATLANTA · SAN FRANCISCO

MACMILLAN AND CO., LIMITED
LONDON · BOMBAY · CALCUTTA
MADRAS · MELBOURNE

THE MACMILLAN COMPANY
OF CANADA, LIMITED
TORONTO

GIVE
JOAN A SWORD

by

SISTER M. THÉRÈSE

of the Congregation of the Sisters of the Divine Savior

Preface

by

JACQUES MARITAIN

New York
THE MACMILLAN COMPANY
1945

Nihil obstat: H. B. Ries, Censor librorum

Imprimatur: ✠ Moyses E. Kiley, Archiepiscopus Milwaukiensis

Die 1 Octobris, 1943

PRINTED IN THE UNITED STATES OF AMERICA
BY THE VAIL-BALLOU PRESS, INC., BINGHAMTON, N. Y.

To

MY BROTHER
priest of God
at whose side I walked
the streets of the Eternal City

For permission to reprint the poems in this book the author wishes to thank the editors of *America, The Catholic World, The Commonweal, The Magnificat, The Saturday Review of Literature, The Savior's Call, The Sign, Spirit,* and *Young Catholic Messenger.*

Like acknowledgment is due the E. P. Dutton Company, New York, N.Y., for permission to reprint "Port-of-Call," "Christmas in Carmel," and "To a Nun-Stigmatist," from *In Praise of Nuns,* edited by James M. Hayes; and The Tower Press, Milwaukee, Wisconsin, for "Wings," from *Choral Speaking Technique* by Agnes Curren Hamm, and "Hummel Pilgrims," from *Berta Hummel, Artist of Innocence,* by Clare Quirk Riedl.

PREFACE

Sister Mary Thérèse's poems convey to us the pure breath of a deep religious inspiration enclosed in the forms of a reverential, subtle and airy song.

It seems to me that a scarcely perceptible vibration in these fluid, translucid lines, betrays the inner tension of the poet's soul, in which the violence of a burning flame of feeling and insight blends with the sweetness and calm of the divine rule. Exquisite freshness and gravity are the fruit of such a lofty peace, which the world cannot give.

What touches me particularly in these poems is that spontaneity, that childlike grace and freedom which unexpectedly surprise and charm the heart: a spiritual liberty that is centered in the fervent quietude of contemplation. Then I think of Coventry Patmore's unforgettable words: "All life and joy is motion. That of time and vulgar souls is linear, and so not without change of place; and good to them is known only in the coming and going. With souls of grace it is not so. They go about a centre, which planetary motion is their joy. They have also a self-revolving motion, which is their pace. Their own regularity enables them to perceive the order of the universe. Their ears with inmost delectation catch the sound of the revolving spheres. They live in fruition of the eternal novelty."

How can the suffering of the world and the cry of the oppressed and the horror of iniquity fail to penetrate to the depths of the spirit of a poet inspired by divine charity? "Give Joan a Sword," Sister Mary Thérèse demands. And she weeps over Paris and its cathedral humiliated by barbarians, and she prays to the Lady of Paris for Her tortured people. May I express the gratitude of a Frenchman for this ardent compassion—and the gratitude of a Thomist for the lovely description which the poet gives us of that "Thomistic revival," at the sight of which

> *she heard a laugh in heaven,*
> *strong footsteps down the sky.*

Jacques Maritain
New York, September, 1943

CONTENTS

GIVE JOAN A SWORD

GIVE JOAN A SWORD

The night is down on Domrémy,
Dark wings have circled every tree,
Shut out the stars and steeped the sky
In anguish lifted like a cry.

Shaking the young stars from her gown,
Pushing the moon back, Joan peers down
On lands by terror twisted bare
That shake with battle everywhere.

A blight is on the world again;
A blight is in the souls of men;
And dark is death and dark is birth
As sorrow runs along the earth.

How can she keep her soul in calm
When towers of Rheims and Notre Dame
Send up their cry of muted bells
That tear her heart with moans and knells?

How must her hands have ached to hold
Her shining sword when pain patrolled
The glory-riddled crimson shore
Of Bataan, and Corregidor.

How must her lips have burned to cry
A challenge to the southern sky
For heroes who would never see
The sunset stain the Coral Sea.

3

Young Joan is restless in the sky;
Young Joan is burning to defy
The sign that sickens men with pride;
Back to the wars young Joan would ride!

To rout this bitter pagan horde,
O God of peace, give Joan a sword!
And in this moment send her down
To Domrémy, to every town!

SKY-RAID

Wings over Paris,
Wings over Rome,
Sinister shadows
On spire and dome.

Wings on the harbor
In the grey dawn
Giving one wisdom
To think upon.

But fiercer pinions
Riding the air
Are the swift spirit's
Hot wings of prayer.

Wings undimensioned
By weight of steel—
Faith is the rudder,
Love is the wheel.

Wings of a people
Valiant and strong
Who will take heaven,
Take it with song!

Let there be no sound
In the dawn's cup
But the soft whirring
Of souls lifted up.

Shatter the star-ways,
Break through the sky,
Every archangel
Is your ally.

Justice your breastplate,
Courage your sword,
With Joan the warrior
Battle the Lord.

Till He send freedom
Fresh from the sky,
Keep your soul flying!
Keep your heart high!

NOTRE DAME DE PARIS

Not that my fathers worshipped in your aisles
Did my heart seek you as the moth the star;
Only for love I came with crying soul
To find the lyric loveliness you are.

I saw your beauty in the summertime—
Each plinth and parapet divinely caught
In a light swirl of doves, your queenly towers
Two white similitudes of purest thought.

I climbed your tower and stood beneath your bell,
Sweet shaken bell that tolled the ages in
To sing the ancient chant of victory,
Or beg for mercy in the battle-din.

I crossed your portal in a day of sun;
I found the love I sought, yet failed to trace
The hint of bitter weeping in the sky,
The damp of human tears upon your face.

For now beneath your towers the desolate go
Seeking some little, pitiful place to hide
From steel wings dropping dust of scarlet pain,
Lady of Paris, spread your mantle wide!

Lean to the wistful children on the quay,
Lean to the limpid silver of the Seine
Where Joan's sweet dust still pleads in every wave,
Lady of Paris, keep the gate, Amen.

THERE IS A CITY LOVELIER

Mary did not keep the gate.
The enemy came through;
And why they tramped her lovely streets
Only the angels knew.

Joan did not wield her shining sword,
Nor did her sweet hands heal
The fissure in each shaken heart
That heard the ringing steel.

No angel threatened at her towers
To hold the wings at bay
That darkened every stone and spire
Upon that bitter day.

O beautiful and lonely one,
What have your saints to tell?
Where was your little shepherdess
The day your beauty fell?

There is a city lovelier,
Under divine patrol,
Across the humblest of its stones
The invader never stole.

And there were towers that did not fall,
And skies they did not climb,
Splendid and tall and radiant,
Forever in their prime.

And there were gates that held that day
Against an evil blight,
Keeping the soul of ancient France
Inviolate as light.

There were the Virgin and Saint Joan
Above the battle cry;
There were the kings and Genevieve
With banners lifted high.

That golden city never fell
Beneath the foe's control—
It is the glowing heart of France,
It is her living soul!

SEASCAPE

Upon the stern an angel,
An angel at the bow,
Starboard and port, an angel
And one at watch below.

For none can know the hour,
Or whether night or day
That death shall walk the water
Atop the crystal spray.

The gulls fly up together
In gleaming grey patrol,
But who has loved the ocean
Knows terror in his soul.

There is no human tower
Of ultimate defense
When hate shall run like fire
In rash improvidence.

Only is sanctuary
Beneath God's harbor-light;
Each weary human spirit
Is precious in His sight.

And death comes gowned in mercy,
With holy chrism signed,
For that her touch is tender,
For that her hands are kind.

The angels drop like blossoms
Loosed from infinity
To lay their bodies gently
In places of the sea.

At bow and stern an angel
With star-enchanted rod;
Bright pinions curving upward
To lift their souls to God.

WINGS

On blue odysseys of sky
Wings have soared and drifted by
Since the tired world began,
Luring, teasing, tempting man;
Till beneath some bright control
Keyed to rhythms of his soul
That would venture sky and sea
Searching for infinity,
Man has dared the lyric trail
Of the lark and nightingale
And with spirit lifted high
Made him splendid wings to fly.

Tempered to a discipline
He had bent his soul to win—
Silver tracks to travel by
In a wilderness of sky—
Taut, austere, divinely kind
Singing concepts of his mind,
From their shining ambuscade
Came the wings that man had made.

From our western shores they flew,
Wind and stars for retinue,
Doves of peace through heaven's blue arc
Dark to dawn, and dawn to dark.
I have seen their whirring host
On the sea-whipped Cornish coast
Swing to south, and swirl again

Over towers that crown the Seine;
And where fluted marbles lean
In the moonlight, I have seen
Old Soracte lift his head
At their still-poised beauty spread
Like a symbol in the air
Of man's spirit tense in prayer
At the world's last terminal.
Flying wings are beautiful!

But when beauty shall rescind
On the burden of the wind,
All your heart will break to know
Bitter ways that wings may go—
Wings with glory on their breath
Dropping loneliness and death,
And from torn wakes in the sky
With a shudder and a cry
Plummeting like stricken things
With no relevance to wings.

Spread no targe against the rain
Of this wild and twisted pain;
Futile will each cover be
Laid on land, on sky and sea;
But at sorrow in the sky
Lift your spirit with a cry—
God of skyways and of men,
Make wings beautiful again!

WRITE IT UPON THE STARS

(On hearing the report that laymen in nazi-occupied Poland may carry the Eucharist and administer it to the sick and dying)

This is the first of the Divine reprisals—
Write it upon the margin of the year
That when our days are told in some far epoch
The splendor of its shining may appear:

As the first Christians bore the precious manna
Into the twisted thoroughfares of men,
So now the simple poor, the unanointed
May touch, and hold, and carry Christ again.

Out of the catacombs of desolation,
The pain-flecked sky, the terror-tunneled sea
They come, a ministry unarmed, defenceless,
Steeled to the stature of divinity.

Christopher bearing Christ across the water,
Tarcisius running down a Roman street,
Carried no braver hearts than these who vanquished
Still hold their spirit poised against defeat.

When pain lifts nations like a grail to heaven
They will cup God, and peace for every pang—
This is the mystery of crucifixion—
On each lone cross a living Christ shall hang.

14

Write it upon the stars, the sun, the planets,
Without the need of metaphor or art—
This is a priesthood sorrow has anointed,
With laurel on its brow, Christ on its heart!

SOLESMES

(After the nazi occupation)

Where dark leaves in a garden
Swirled upward with a cry—
An old monk walked, a shadow
Between the earth and sky.

The young monks had departed
To choirs on sea and air
Where strong psalms fall like meteors
Along the battle flare.

But here was desolation,
A bitter interval—
The song of centuries muted
To pain's antiphonal.

Was it a dream upon him?
Was it the chant he heard
In supple rhythms rising
Like notes of a sky-flung bird?

Its roots were in a singing
That coiled about his heart,
The mystic vine of Godhead
Of which he was a part.

And though his soul was tortured
And stretched upon a tree,
His flesh was quick with music,
His veins ran deity.

16

He felt each cooling cadence
Leap to his lips and rise
Above the ancient towers
That soared into the skies.

A melismatic pattern
In love's modality
Leaped like a text of David
Vibrant with prophecy:

Though armies stand in battle
And camp along the walls,
Strong psalms shall rise forever
From out the heart's taut stalls

And from the soul's bright towers,
From restless dusk to dawn—
Thus will the song be endless,
Thus will the chant go on!

LILIES MORE THAN BREAD

(For a philanthropist)

Go not empty-hearted
Into the marts of men,
The brightest coin will darken
And lose its lustre when
The hand that gives is loveless
And folds in pride again.

There is a spirit-hunger
Sharper than body's need;
There is an infinite thirsting
For cups of wisdom's mead;
While on the rim of laughter
A stricken heart may bleed.

With bread and cooling water
The body's feast is spread;
Not so the straining spirit's
That will be housed and fed
By love more than a roof-tree,
And lilies more than bread.

THOMISTIC REVIVAL

Down the cool corridor
I saw a friar pass
Not on his way to Prime,
Not on his way to Mass.

Nor to some ancient hall
Of the Angelicum
Where medieval-gowned
Close-tonsured scholars come.

This is a modern town;
Beauty wears no disguise;
Most unconventual
Gay girls with eager eyes

Resolve no more to stand
At wisdom's postern gate,
But storm its shining towers
With coup importunate.

The torch which Maritain
Re-trimmed in Aquin's name
Fair hands would carry high,
Fling wide its living flame.

Pert curls, incredible hats,
Mask their bright stratagem;
Hyde Park and Union Square
Straightway shall hear from them.

Some sombre-hooded scribe
Might stare, be shocked and vexed,
Hearing sweet voices run
Along his limpid text,

But he to whom his Lord
Said, "Thou hast written well,"
Over his parchment page
Would chuckle in his cell,

Lay down his feathered quill,
Swift drop upon his knees,
"Lord, let me leap the years
To tutor such as these!"

When past my door today
A white-robed friar went by,
I heard a laugh in heaven,
Strong footsteps down the sky.

WHO WOOS A DOVE

WHO WOOS A DOVE

"Whatever we can do to hasten the day when the dove
of peace may find on this earth, submerged in a deluge of
discord, somewhere to alight, we shall continue to do . . ."
(*Summi Pontificatus,* First Encyclical of Pope Pius XII)

She who was late a bright-winged, luminous bird
Is now a mourning dove, remote and plain;
Widowed of joy, she wheels a piteous flight
Above the bitter, whirling tides of pain.

Or poises cross-wise, hung against the sky,
Pressed to the four blue winds in last retreat;
How may she find some place of quietude
Where only grief may walk with naked feet?

Is none to woo her back? Be comforted.
Her wings are fettered by invisible snares
Held by a hand too beautiful to touch,
Whose fingers taper to a thousand prayers.

Who woos this dove wears peace upon his brow,
Love is the latch, the lintel of his door,
For her he trysts with mercy in the dusk,
And lies the lonely night upon the floor.

The stricken voices of the martyred North
Cry in his soul with pleading to be fed;
And unattended in the dawn he goes
To pour for them the wine, and break the bread.

23

The peoples of the Southland, East, and West,
From purpled kings to lowliest of men
Are tissue of his soul, to his serene
Unfrontiered heart, no heart is alien.

For them he woos the dove with pitiful word
That she must hear wherever she may hide;
His heart goes crying past the uttermost star,
His arms are wide with love as God's are wide.

Until some sudden morning he shall rise,
Throw wide the shutters to the sun-rinsed air,
And know that laughter runs upon the sea,
Joy on the hills, with April in her hair.

That flutes of dawn along the colonnades
Flutter with music of eternal springs—
An olive branch will lie upon the sill,
And at his listening heart, the beat of wings.

PRAYER FOR THE PONTIFF

(Pope Pius XII)

God, set no boundaries to his love who came
Softly upon that dusk-hung balcony
And with love's urgent art
Gathered a derelict world up to his heart;
An aching, wistful world that lately heard
The stirrings of a holy bird
Bearing an olive branch, then swift as flame
Upon the wind, the music of a name—
Eugenio!—like shaken bells adrift—
And nations knelt to take his lips' first glowing gift,
As vibrant, warm
And cruciform,
It swept the world with blessing, healing death's late rift.

He is no stranger, God, for whom we pray
And lift this word today.
His feet have walked our land
Coming upon the winds and on the sea
Bearing Christ's courtesy.
And we have known the pressure of his hand,
The peace of his embrace,
And unaware
Have seen him kneel in lonely prayer,
Your light upon his face.

Then hear his cry
What times his eager hands are lifted up
Prayer-worn and beautiful against the dawn

In suppliance for his sheep;
Give him the years of peace he dreams upon,
Whose soul glows as a quenchless flame,
Whose lips are lyric with a nameless Name,
Whose fingers burn to bind
The throbbing wounds of human-kind,
Whose arms are wide to comfort all who weep.

Grant him his strongest prayer:
That from the bitter waters of despair
The nations swift rise up
And from his white hands take the mystic loving cup
With fealty no hurtling fear can break;
Leaving the ancient ache
Of greed of land and power, for Justice's sake
And love's, crush barriers man's hate has flung
To the mute stars, and deeply sorrow-stung,
Stretch golden girders over earth's distress
With words that heal and bless;
That by the dusk some arch of peace may span
The enmities that sever man from man;
Lest where the poppy flowers weep in the rain
Fragile and lovely lives again be slain;
While on some tattered mountain peak
God's frightened children cry their hearts to sleep.

God, give him strength
When he shall sound the breadth, the depth, and length
Of mankind's inhumanity;
In stark Gethsemane

Let not his heart break on some agony,
But straightway mold
Some cup of comfort for his hands to hold,
And pitiful, send an angel down to share
The keen, tense terror of his wordless prayer.

Let serried troops disband,
And with the trust of children take his hand,
For not with battle-song, and beat of drums,
But gently, unarmed, strong in faith, he comes,
An angel-shepherd in a mystic shroud,
Stooping to bind the broken wing
Of each bereft, bewildered, wounded thing;
An anxious shepherd with a staff that leans
Heavy upon his hand until it fold
And gather home
From the four winds of heaven the sheep that roam;
His shining mind
By holy wisdom signed,
Subduing life's complexities
To love's ineffable unities.

God, give him light
To lead his flock through shadow of this night
Into the pastures of infinity;
Past burnished parapets and saffron towers
Into the summer meadows warm with flowers,
Where, let there be fulfilled
What You have willed
To still man's hunger-cry:

One fold, one Shepherd under the wide sky!
Each wistful sheep by his swift mercy, fed.
Each whimpering lambkin lifted to its bed.
And all the tired world divinely comforted.

INCIDENT IN THE HALL OF BENEDICTIONS

The colonnades were gold with sun,
Through arches laced with light
A soft sirocco stirred the plumes
Of prince and noble knight
Who waited in the motley crowd
A vision robed in white.

The voices rose as golden mist
Before a lifted throne;
The eyes that leaned to meet your eyes
Were for your soul alone,
While eucharists of blessing fell
Like blossoms heaven-blown.

Within the Father's house is peace.
One walks with certain grace,
As if an angel caught your hand
And smiled into your face;
Even a child may lift its voice
So holy is the place.

Viva il Papa! with a cry
In cadence sweet as death
A small voice took the limpid notes,
The magic shibboleth,
That as a subtle wonder hung
On such a fragile breath.

Only the Pontiff's mystic soul
And shaken heart could know

Where in that flood of lyric sound
Was luminous undertow,
Or why the cool voice of a child
Could ever hunger so.

The pilgrims went to North and South,
And over the blue sea-rim,
Each pilgrim carried in his soul
A sight no years can dim:
A child upon its mother's arm,
A smile of seraphim.

The Caesars sleep in mellow dust
In marble disarray,
Their villas crumble on the hills
Where cypress moan and sway;
And yet their brows were never bright
As is this child's today.

Though diadems encrust the years
With jeweled emphasis,
Not any crown this child may wear
Will ever shine as this:
Upon its forehead like a star—
The holy Pontiff's kiss.

FOR A DEAD CANARY—(Caged in the Vatican)

By what bright skeins of song, what invisible tether
Was bound to heaven's will
This spilling of sun, this crumpled bloom of feather
Golden upon the sill?

While young birds sang in the hills, your innocent duty
Was to poise on a golden swing
And from quivering throat trill notes of a delicate beauty
For earth's most lovely king.

From over the dome the doves dipped low to hear it
Fall from its marble height,
The luminous psalm you laid against his spirit
Each dawn and southern night.

And you were content with this simple song, this tender
Lyric contemplative,
Till you heard the song in his heart, an aching splendor
No bird could bear and live.

Had I known of your piteous plight I had told you the won-
der,
But my tall ship sailed away—
And dreams are ghosts—so your small heart broke asunder
Hearing it day by day.

A little bird is with rapture unacquainted,
Unlearned in mystic lore;
A haloed face, the touch of fingers sainted,
You never knew before.

So you laid your singing by, and your heart broke gladly
In the dark of that lonely room.
Now I hear over winds of two seas the report—and sadly—
Of crumpled golden bloom.

I SEND OUR LADY

I SEND OUR LADY

I may not venture to your door
And lift the latch, as I would do;
I send Our Lady in my stead
Tonight, to comfort you.

(For in the smiling of your eyes
I feel the dark where tears have lain,
Under the music of your voice,
The counterpoint of pain.)

Beneath the February moon,
A lithe, cool crescent in the sky,
She will be haloed regally
As she goes softly by.

In the white vigil of your prayer
Under the lintel she will tread
And know you by the curving light
You wear about your head.

She will shut out philosophy;
Lay your bright wisdom on the sill;
For there are caverns in the soul
That only love can fill—

Stark intervals of silence, when
Even the spirit poised in grace
Is chastened by the pity worn
Upon a woman's face.

Beyond the touch of any thought
Or little word that she may speak,
Will be the solace of her arms,
Her kiss upon your cheek.

And from my window at the dawn
My soul will fly like any bird
To nestle at her heart, and hear
The music she has heard.

FRA ANGELICO'S ANNUNCIATION

(In the monastery of San Marco, Florence)

Upon this casual stretch of cloister wall
Five troubled centuries ago
The subtle hand of Fra Angelico
Limned beauty beyond name
To sear the soul, tunnel the heart with flame.
Here might an Aquin kneel
And make appeal;
Or some blithe novice venturous and gay
Slipping from psalms to play
Pause at this ancient door
To kneel heart-shaken on the worn grey floor;
Or a grave friar fevered with a mood
For dialectics, coming unaware
Up this brief stair
Might lift his snowy hood
And cool his soul in prayer.

A girl in contemplation bent;
Tall Gabriel on a strange wooing sent
Who, struck at this tremendous thing
Stirs to the last bright feather of his wing;
It were a simpler thing to break the skies
Like lightning, but to meet this maiden's eyes
Blue-wet as dawn, as unperplexed,
Even an angel might forget his text;
But she with woman's quickened sense
Noting his heavenly diffidence
Leans sweetly toward him, unafraid—

Yet coy as any maid—
To reassure her shining cavalier
There is no need for fear.
Then as his archangelic eloquence
Untrammeled of suspense
Bursts on her spirit like a summer storm
Her breath comes quick and warm,
And with a start,
As if all heaven presses on her heart
She sees the angel in a golden blur,
And knows within her flesh a new life stir.

Nor Giotto's lily-tower, nor Tuscan sun
Gold on the Arno lures my heart for long,
Nor Dante and the woman of his song—
But I would ride
The perilous seas again for one small grace—
To kneel one moment only in that place
And rapturously see
Beneath a curving canopy
Bright Gabriel, his every feather stirred;
A listening girl encompassing the Word.

ON SEEING MURILLO'S PAINTING OF THE
IMMACULATE CONCEPTION IN THE LOUVRE

This is the great Murillo's dream of her—
A Lady poised upon the moon's white arc;
Without a blot or blur
Set heaven-wise
On burnished pigment of his Spanish skies;
About her pose of state
Blown rhythms of angels undulate
And lift her mystically apart
Holding some infinite secret to her heart.
And I, a captive to her human grace
Stand in the cool glint of Parisian noon
Wrapt beyond time and space.
But soon, too soon
Am I distraught
With a vague trifle of incongruous thought:
I am a child again, waking at night
Mute with the dark and fright
Who sees a moon-washed picture on the wall—
Murillo's Lady sweet and tall—
And I remember with a sudden stir
How all my frightened heart went out to her
And framed bewilderingly
A small wild wish to be
Of all the little angels tumbling down,
That roguish cherub hiding in her gown.

SALUTE

(Before the statue of Our Lady of Peace in St. Mary Major)

The little lad brushed past me like a dart
Thrown by some seraph lurking in the gloom
Pushing the opal dusk apart
At arch and chiseled tomb;
Where down the tall nave's pillared road
Bright Hymettus marble glowed
This little one
With sweet face bronzed by an Italian sun
Came to a crisp halt where
A white madonna waited wistfully
For some small prayer,
Or still word spoken to her Child
Who held an olive branch, and smiled.

With ritual of medieval knight
Taut at attention, drawn to his full height,
This cherubic recruit
Raised a small hand in swift salute
As it were meet
That he salute a lady in the street,
So now this Lady in the dusk-dimmed nave
Beneath the multi-shadowed architrave.

But as he turned to go I saw him start
As at some little thought that bruised his heart—
Had he heard what the blue winds said
Of bitter steel wings overhead?—
Oblivious of discipline

This military mannikin
In one swift bound
Climbed to her feet,
And heedless of the worshippers' critique
Leaned close across the rhythms of her gown
And laid a kiss upon her curved, cool cheek,
Then scrambled down
And fleet
Fled through the pillars to the Roman street.

As when a tired tree against a hill
Is rinsed with sudden music and grows still,
So stood I spirit-shaken, pondering
The lonely wisdom of this thing:
Not only in lip-rubric told with care
Is power of prayer;
There is a luminous leaven
Of silence more articulate to bless—
There are some things that must be torn from heaven
By tears and tenderness.

GALILEAN MAY

Into the hills of Galilee
Our Lady went one day
Lured by the wonder-woven bloom
Dropped from the looms of May.

Slim lilies leaned to touch her gown.
Curving through delicate air
A fledgling thrush flew to her hand,
Butterflies to her hair.

She told her secret to the winds
That brushed her garment hem,
The tear-wet pitying winds that blew
Up from Jerusalem.

And as she spoke a little name
Tremulous, low and sweet,
A golden surf of buttercups
Broke against her feet.

The winds and flowers of Galilee
Grown wistful of her face
Still wait her footfall at the May—
Gentle, and full of grace.

I GO TO BETHLEHEM

When the shepherds' tired feet are still,
And the sheep have crept back over the hill,
Quietly I shall go down
Along the road to David's town
Looking for one I know is here,
Who went this way with a touch of fear,
Who may need a word to calm her stress,
And the strength of a woman's tenderness.

It is a cave I stand before;
A lantern is set outside the door—
No light is needed within this place,
There is light enough on the young girl's face—
I enter noiselessly, unheard,
And kneel beside her without a word;
This is a night past joy, past tears,
A night that is as a thousand years.
My hands are empty, for this brief bliss
I can but give her my lips to kiss,
For in lonely days that the years now hide
I shall need her beauty at my side.
But the joy of which her heart is full
Is infinitely multiple,
And the child that made her body light
I shall carry with me into the night.

When the last bright star is swinging low
You too may come across the snow
And with a heart and spirit free

43

Kneel in the rugged cave with me;
Not as the kings, with pomp and stir,
Bringing their gold, incense and myrrh;
At a timid knock the door swings wide,
The merest beggar may step inside,
With never a song and never a gem
You may go down to Bethlehem,
And for a gift on Christmas day
You too may carry the child away.

A FOUNTAIN SEALED

One brief phrase out of scripture I prefer
To other praise of her—

She was a woman who had learned the art
Of pondering in her heart.

Of inner cherishing, keeping the word
By which her soul was stirred.

Beneath the literal integument
She sweetly bent

To inner meanings, limpid and profound,
That held her bound

To them for all the years that she should be,
Tasting their ecstasy.

Much as the fleeting color of a wing
Might hold one pondering,

Or poignant words of lovers, told apart
Still rend the heart.

This is the woman I would stand before
At Nazareth's unlatched door.

This is the radiant woman I would meet
On Bethlehem's narrow street,

Serenely poised and beautifully wise,
Whose soul burns in her eyes

Holding its secret wisdom, love-annealed,
As a fountain sealed.

TRAVEL NOTE

TRAVEL NOTE

This is journey to be made
In a sun-rinsed southern noon;
But if dappled heavens lend
Courtesy of star and moon

Take the night by mountain way
Luminous into Tuscany;
Ride in moonlight through the hills,
Ride in moonlight to the sea.

Listen at Verona's gate—
Nightingale and blossom yet
In her ancient citadel
Whimper over Juliet.

Lean to hear the Arno tell
Silver word of night like this
When beside her waters came
The immortal Beatrice.

Or on Umbrian cloister wall
Glimpse the olive's white festoon
Shining like a matin prayer
Lovely in a night of moon.

Let them steal your heart away:
Cypress and star-clutching pines
Standing tip-toe to the sky
On the moon-washed Apennines.

When across some Roman road
One pink sprig of almond nods,
Take the hand of destiny,
Enter Latium with the gods.

FIRST MASS IN THE CATACOMBS

Here where the Popes have lain them down
And found their resting sweet,
Over the dust of ancient stones
You come with eager feet

In robes as scarlet as their blood
Who loved this silver gloom,
Whose names are music on the walls
Across each marble tomb.

Where grey vaults lay a tender mist
On a carrara scroll
Where lyric Damasus has spilled
A cadence of his soul

There is a simple table laid
Within the crypt's dim light;
There is a cup of vintage set,
A host-crust round and white.

The centuries crumble at a breath;
The brittle days are dumb
As down the shadowed corridors
The early Christians come.

We kneel together on the stones,
Gently you break the bread,
It is the olden banquet rite
And all who come are fed.

A new-anointed seals again
Love's ageless unity,
Soft voices answer through the dusk
The ancient liturgy.

Love keeps her luminous, mystic tryst
The years, the centuries long—
And there where tall Cecilia lay
There is a golden song.

THIS KNITTING OF SOULS

(In memory of a First Mass in the Catacombs)

I lost my heart to her hills and her pointed cypress;
I tethered my soul, an untamed drifting thing
To the strength of her stern, wind-buffeted campaniles
To be torn by a tossing bell, or bruised by a wing.

Her moon-wet marbles have left a song within me;
Rome! the mere touch of her name's eternity
Still gives a stress to my feet to run swift-sandaled
The long white road from Ostia and the sea.

We are remade by a love within the spirit.
Yet of such loves as have seared and refashioned me quite—
Footprints of martyrs, clear bells, hands newly-anointed—
One is a poignance against my heart tonight.

One moment caught from a brief and golden summer
When your eyes were lit with a strange and sudden flame
And I felt the warmth of your soul as I walked beside you
Over the stones of that city of deathless name.

Long deep tunnels of gloom in the earth's dark bosom
Winnowed with light never native to sea or to land—
Limpid light from a cup that is brimming and throbbing,
Light from a snowy disc you hold in your hand.

Centuries melt like a mist with this sun upon them—
Sun of the Christ-life that binds us, the Christ-light that
    brings

The ancient beautiful dead with their nimbused faces
Here where the Pontiffs kneel and Cecilia sings.

Castles and hills, and song in the earth's dark places
Shall pass some day from my spirit and not return,
But never this knitting of souls in a mystic oneness
At your morning altar where two candles burn.

AT THE CRYPT OF SAINT CECILIA

(Catacombs of Saint Callixtus, Rome)

I am no pilgrim on this Appian way.
Unfettered of each formal-mannered mode
I am a little child gone out to play
With sandals twinkling on the cobbled road,
Skipping along the cypress shadows, free
From wheels upon the highway hurrying by
Over the blue campagna to the sea,
With Rome a muted murmur on the sky.

It is so holy and so hushed a thing
To leave the sun and slip into the gloom,
To call, and hear Cecilia answering,
And find her waiting in this little room
With gifts—love like a light, pain like a dart,
And song a luminous weight upon the heart.

COLISEUM

What wisdom stayed our feet
That we should meet
Here where the ancient street
Circles these arches looped against the sky?
There were a hundred places one might wait—
The cypress walk, Sebastian's gate,
Or where the low door breaks the ivied wall
Into the vineyards, yet
As if in answer to some inner call
Here on the mellow stones we are well met.

Within the shadow of no other place
Could I more truly read your face—
For in a lonely hour
Out of the ruddy crust
Of this sweet dust
Leaped living leaf and flower,
Bloom that has brightly blown
Long centuries, nor ever known
Time's withering loss,
Bloom that in bitter rain
Measured its blossoming by one stark cross,
And dying bore the ripened fruit of pain.

That wheel of swallows through the crumbling arches,
That fall of doves on the last broken tier,
The mounting summer sun that burns and parches
The stone to gold, mark the austere
Bright token

Our lips exchange upon this sacred street
Pressed by the martyrs' feet;
Knowing the mystic-circle is unbroken—
Still in each soul that strives and gives
Love intimately lives;
Still in the vibrant flesh is sacrificed
The lovely limbs of Christ.

Here where beneath a bitter tread
The golden wheat was ground to holy bread,
Here where the first fruit of the living Vine
Was crushed to wine,
Begin your journey into love, and ride
Seas that stretch perilously
Wide as your heart is wide!
With luminous certainty
Let all who meet you on the way
Know we have met upon these stones today.

ROMAN EVENING

To south—a young moon on the sea's blue border
Curved like a golden tusk;
To east—the first importunate star of evening
Dancing upon Soracte in the dusk;
From Tusculum to Ostia a rainbow
Pressed firmly on the west;
Love is abroad tonight and walking the skyways
On an ancient quest.

Place a hush on your heart, a calm on your spirit,
Make wide the door—
Set a tall taper in your eastern window,
A small stool on the floor.
Then wait with a breathless awe, a wordless wonder,
Each sound of living thinned
To a single cry as the air turns bright and golden
With Christ's words on the wind.

OVER LAKE ALBANO

Here is a peace that passes understanding—
From this cool balcony
The lake is yours, cupped in its emerald crater,
Yours are the hills, and yours the singing sea.

You may touch the fluttering stars where Monte Cavo
In his snood of purple sky
Still leans to Latium; pontiffs and emperors
From this stone height have seen her ghosts slip by.

Each push of the waves in the sea-wind, each dark-poised
    cypress
Reflects an artist's skill
Who sits through the infinite years at a glowing canvas
Bending the sunsets and lakes to His infinite will.

Bending the spirit of man to the hush within him
On such full nights as this
When the stillness is weighted with strange, unuttered mu-
    sic,
And a new word stirs in love's bright chrysalis.

Now let the soul-tree wear along its branches
More bloom than April had—
So graced is the human heart with divine awareness
A bird, a song, a star can make it glad.

59

Yet the stars that ride in the waves are but darkened mir-
    rors,
Shadows, as Plato said,
That but hint at the luminous towers in the soul's far city
Where with infinite beauty she shall be comforted.

AT THE MANGER OF BETHLEHEM

(In the crypt of St. Mary Major, Rome)

Under the beat of ancient bells
That break the midnight into canticles,
I kneel and love and wonder like a child—
Dreaming upon a lovely head bent low
Above these little manger boards,
Glad with the sweetest weight a wood can know,
Shadowed by seven swords.

The questioning night, the stars, the song on heaven's sill,
Quaint shepherds from the hill,
A shy blue-mantled maid with one bright Word to keep,
A little Child asleep—
With accurate grace
Each letter of the scripture falls into its place,
Only the setting fails—a world at peace.

Under the beating bells, the uncertain light,
Let the wide world creep here tonight
And gather on the tessellated floor,
The poor, the proud, the spirit-maimed, the whole,
Each with his lonely soul;
If all our peace must start
In the disputed country of the heart,
It is the hour to kneel
And make appeal.

Within this holy night there shall not lack
Love's pity and compassion, nor a need

61

Remain unfilled, no soul will hurry back
Into some dim pain-riddled street to cede
One moment to despair,
For love shall lie like music on the air—
Where dark armadas huddle in the skies
And shade our searching eyes
The maid of Bethlehem will tread the night
To bind with gentle rite
And mystic cincture to this crib again
The anguished race of men,
To lift her Child to bless
Their loneliness,
Setting her smile in heaven as symbol of release,
And one great dazzling star to tell of peace.

YOU WILL COME BACK

Into the pool of Trevi
Toss a coin tonight.
It is a magic symbol;
It is an ancient rite.

And as the waters tremble,
Ripple and move apart,
A weight of soft enchantment
Will settle on your heart.

The rhythms of your spirit
Will leap to crest and swoon
Under a star-etched heaven,
Under a Roman moon.

The angel of the fountain
Who reads your heart tonight
Will spin a spell about you
And weave a web of light.

And little will it matter
What boundaries there be,
Or what fair ship shall take you
Across whatever sea,

For his voice will lure you ever
Over the woods and rills
Back to this queen of cities
Couched on her seven hills.

You cannot choose but follow—
And with all your sails unfurled
You will come back a pilgrim
Over the rim of the world.

TREE-CHANT

(In the hillside cemetery at Lisieux)

Beneath our many-dappled shade
The lovely child Teresa played,
Gathering cornflowers by the wall
And daisies tall as she was tall;
She wore a light about her face—
A light of wisdom and of grace,
Her eyes glowed with a holy spark,
Her voice soared upward like a lark.

This beauty blooming swift and still
Lured heaven down to earth, until
At Carmel in the valley there
They laid a veil upon her hair.
The days were long, the years were long,
We missed her smile and missed her song,
But saw a star of golden light
Above her window every night.

One Norman dawn when winds were chill
They brought her gently up the hill—
A rose from summer's diadem,
A lily broken on its stem.
We laid soft winds upon her bed,
And autumn stars about her head.

But in the years we heard her stir—
The little leaves that covered her
Thrilled upward startled at the sight

Of maid uprising, gowned in light,
Who took the road by thrushes purled,
The road that led to all the world.

In pity of our lonely plight
They say she walks the hill at night,
Grown beautiful, and blithe, and tall,
And gathers roses by the wall;
Then from her bright sill in the sky
To each small prayer and lifted cry
She drops them gently down again
Into the waiting souls of men.

IN WESTMINSTER ABBEY

(In the east walk of the cloisters, near the chapter-house,
long ago a little girl was buried. Her tomb bears the simple
inscription, "Jane Lister, dear childe.")

Here with the poets' dust and dust of kings
I sought for you that day,
Questioned each shadow in the storied nave
To find the place you lay.
In chapels paved with princes I leaned low
To scan each marble row,
Searching the tombs of king and queen
To see if a small child had crept between.
Beneath the old south transept's lyric line
I sought a word or sign—
But Chaucer's singing dust slept on unstirred,
Spenser would speak no word,
Nor any jeweled queen bend down to tell
The secret of your cell.

A thousand thoughts about you tore my heart—
You who were part
Of summer wind, of robin-song, of light,
Must surely be
Lonely among this dignity;
Heaven pitying you, upon an April day
Perhaps an angel came
Through the long gloom and called your name
Inviting you to come and play
At hide-and-seek, or butterfly,

But with a caution in his eye
To romp the chancels softly lest you waken
A casual queen, or kingly dust be shaken.
Had Handel's soaring soul unloosed in spring
Some gay young melody for you to sing?
Or had you grown by grace
Contemplative, these long grey centuries through
Having no other thing to do
But talk to God within this ancient place?

Where quaint prayers burn along the walls, I sought
And found you not.

But in the cloisters where the old monks lie
Swathed in their long cloaks, smiling at the sky—
A merry company
Where any wondering child would love to be—
There where the stars have worn the grey walls thin,
I found the little stone that locks you in.

At ultimate trumpet-call
When moons will melt and sun and stars will fall;
When fold on fold of royal dust will rise—
The saint, the nobly wise,
No king shall claim the day
Nor comely queen dispute your sway
As through the abbey's shattered wall
Little Jane Lister, you shall lead them all
At the archangel's nod
Skipping and singing up the clouds to God.

PORT-OF-CALL

(Passing Spain, September 1939)

A quiver of wings and the gulls dip into the sunset,
My heart leans with them to starboard eagerly
As spectral and stark the sierras of Andalusia
Rise from a sun-flecked sea.

We pause at no port for the seas are sown with peril;
We shall trail the dark through the pillars of Hercules;
But the human soul may leap the waves unfettered
Of such contingencies

To this land of the Moor, the mystic, the bright-robed
    martyr,
Of John the seraphic, whose soul was a lonely flame;
But my heart cries out to that greatest of all her women
A thousand Carmels name.

I walk the streets still sweet with the press of her sandals,
The winding paths that re-echo the petulant beat
Of her mule's small hoofs, as Teresa rode into the morning
In the wake of the Paraclete.

I kneel at her side by the little grated window
And feel the hot pulse of her prayer, the divine instress
Of a love that she followed with passionate, wild abandon
Through streets of bitterness.

I thrill at the words that have told me of all her doctrine
Of what rich fibre her soul, how sternly true—

"Will I open the grill? O Gratian, how little you know me!
I would open my heart to you!"

The shoreline drops within God's bluest ocean;
There are tears on my cheek, and the sky is a misty pall
Where only the silver track of a gull marks eastward
The spirit's port-of-call.

NOT IN THE TEXT OF PLATO

NOT IN THE TEXT OF PLATO

Not in the text of Plato or the sages
Seek for this word
By which the fibre of your soul is stirred.

Nor in the runes of mystics will you find it;
It will evade
The subtlest line that any man has made.

Travail of mind and heart will never win it,
Nor frugal years
Upon a broken crust, and wine of tears.

Children have come upon it in a garden—
A blithesome thing
Spilled in their hearts like quiet rain in spring.

The poor, the humble have been known to hold it
Complete and whole
When the wide winds of love blow through the soul.

The sweet, uncertain moment of its coming
Is God's to keep;
The secret of the King lies very deep.

But when you have been shaken past believing
By pain, by fear,
Know that the blessed time is very near.

And when stark silences close in about you
Too deep to name,
Searing your spirit to a pointed flame,

Know that the days of waiting are accomplished;
In peace unblurred
Kneel in the stillness and receive the Word.

HUMMEL PILGRIMS

How far is it to heaven-town?
Into the valley winding down
You see the long white road we came,
A narrow road without a name.

It must have been but yesterday
We met upon this mountain way,
Gathering crocus left by spring,
Counting the colors on a wing.

For we were told that past the sun—
Whoever is a little one
Will find the good God waiting there
Within a shining house of prayer.

Our basket is a little load;
We join our hands upon the road
And sing the pretty songs we know,
While hurrying toward the peaks of snow.

There is an angel tall and cool
Who winds the wind upon a spool
And trails the blue thread in our way
To mark our journey in the day.

When long night shadows cast a fear,
A lovely Lady walking near
Prepares our bed upon the ground
And with her mantle wraps us round.

Then on a window in the sky
She sets a taper warm and high;
We watch the fluttering light from far
Until it blossoms in a star.

At early dawn we rise from bed,
We share our prayers and share our bread;
We have no fear for anything,
And when we lose the path we sing.

We care not if the road winds high—
Our names are written in the sky!
Nor if the purple hills are wide—
If God lives on the other side!

IN AVILA

The matin chant she scarcely heard;
There was a light about each word
And in her heart a singing bird.

There was no letter she could say;
Nor could she turn her soul away;
And yet by night and yet by day

The very air that wrapped her round
Was wet with coolnesses of sound
Like crystal rivers underground.

There was no place that she could hide—
As easy push the stars aside
As hush the singing in her side.

Song that was sound she could not hear;
Song that was touch she could not fear;
A presence piercing like a spear.

What is this bird that can subdue
The heart, the mind, the spirit too?
Then in a sudden light she knew

Love is the lock and love the key
That opens wide this mystery
Of swift invasion by the Three.

TO A NUN-STIGMATIST

My hand within your hand;
My fingers touch a scar
Etched keener than the night
Cut by the sharpest star.

We spoke of simple things
Meant for the lips alone:
Far lands that I had seen,
Quaint nuns that you had known.

But deep beneath our words
Like song lost in a wood
Your heart cried out to mine,
My spirit understood.

Soul-fibre seared to ash;
Heart bruised and desolate;
This is the secret pact
Of the initiate.

Since on the mystic tree
Blossomed the twisted thorn,
By every several branch
This token must be worn.

There is divine intent
In every wounding thing
That keeps the heart elate,
That makes the spirit sing.

JESSICA TAKES THE VEIL

This is the most perfect poem that she has written—
This script of grace
Etched on the soul's living vellum with love's keen stiletto,
This April flower with the breath of God on its face.

Its white rippling word is no casual song of a moment
Nor decade of years,
The measureless days of the spirit have gone to its making,
Lone midnights of reticent wisdom, of shadow, of tears.

Stripped of the moon and the hills, the bright barter of
cities,
Clean of the sea,
Her song is bent to a beauty lyric within her,
The light and the lantern, the bride and the bride-song is
she.

I know not her face, we have met in the darkness only
On the austere hills of song,
But I know on what roads she has come to this beautiful
morning,
On what rapturous ways she will go that are bitter and long.

Today they will robe the sweet singer in garments befitting
Her bridal of prayer—
The gown the intrepid Teresa has worn before her,
Cool sandals, a mantle to hide her, a veil for her hair.

Each little bird that alights on the sill of Carmel
Will rest his wings,

79

The stars will go begging to peer through her small cell
    window
To see how a mystic prays and a poet sings.

While we shall go weighted with words and blinded with
    seeing
Till the slow heart learns
There are times when the sweetest of music is less than
    silence,
The sun less bright than the dark where a lantern burns.

CHRISTMAS IN CARMEL

(For the nuns of the Carmel of the Mother of God)

Now in this quiet love-illumined night
My wistful soul will be a Carmelite

And at the grill within the holy place
Bend low to gaze upon a Child's small face.

In the blue midnight, underneath the sky,
All of my suppliant soul melts in a cry—

Kindle me with some white Teresian flame,
Who wear the subtle wonder of her name,

That in the marts of men I walk apart
Keeping a cloistered and untroubled heart.

And give me of the gentle Doctor's fire
Who wooed the cross and died of its desire,

That up bright Carmel's mountain I be led,
On crumbs of mystic wisdom comforted.

Then fold within your hands, secure and whole,
The precious loves You knit into my soul.

With this small lifted song my heart I bring
Here to your Carmel cradle, little King.

POET AND BIRD

I hear a little bird sing every morning
With startling unrestraint,
Could he have come from Eden without a taint

That he so bends his heart to this wild rapture—
His being wrapt and wrung
Until the bright weight of his song be sung?

Mine is the sheerest beggary of music
Compared to this
That leaps and lifts beyond analysis.

I must take caution in my briefest singing,
Stripping each line and word
Until but purest melody is heard.

And though the first notes leap like buds in April
By a bright sun kissed,
The summits of my song are hung with mist.

For words are human only, taking their measure
By a sun or a star—
Infinities beneath the things that are.

But just beyond the widest curve of music
One still unuttered line
Is the bright reason of his song and mine.

On some far day we shall win to this ultimate cadence
That holds each being stirred—
Beggar and troubadour, poet and bird.

FOR A BLIND CHILD

Let no one question with surprise
While to the tint of saffron skies
God laid a shadow on your eyes,

Or why white liturgies of dawn
With tulip tapers on the lawn
Your eyes have never looked upon,

Unless he know not of the speech
Of mystery that love can teach;
Beauty the senses cannot reach.

Vision beyond their brief control,
By lamps of luminous aureole
Within the castle of the soul

Where, when the senses' blinds are low,
In gowns of mist, and wings of snow
The little angels come and go.

And you perceive Love's unity
Unblurred by multiplicity;
And you are blessed who cannot see.

Thus life becomes a game all day
At which the little Christ will play
Until He kiss the dark away.

THE HOUSE OF THE SPIRIT

THE HOUSE OF THE SPIRIT

"There are souls . . . that on their first meeting enter the
most holy place . . ."—(A biographer of St. Francis)

This is the house of quiet
The hush of years has made,
To which the human spirit
Ventures unafraid.

No casual hands have lifted
Its walls austere and high,
Nor set its luminous windows
That open to the sky.

To reach this gracious doorway
One must have traveled far—
Through deep mirage of desert,
And nights without a star.

God sets the ways of spirit
Though separate and stark,
In some inscrutable moment
To meet, in sun or dark.

And no one need go lonely
In love's or wisdom's name
If he but steel his spirit,
And rinse his heart with flame.

I searched the golden city
Beneath the Roman pines;

I leaned on cypress-scented
Winds from the Apennines

To catch some hidden music
Where a white footfall stirred,
To feel the darkness broken
By one small mystic word.

And on blue trails of ocean
Through futile, endless space,
I reached for hands to lead me
To this most quiet place.

Then in the dusk I found you
With all your soul for light—
Here at the end of seeking,
Here at the end of night.

Let us go in together
With wonder on our breath,
This bright house of the spirit
Where love is strong as death.

ONE SOUL TO ANOTHER

This is the law of love:
We live and move
And have our being in divinity.
From out this mystery
Flow countless corollaries wide and free:

Christ in us both
One leaping pulse—and we are each to each
Closer than music to the strings, than word to speech.

When from some mystic bowl
You drain the bitter wine,
Soul of my soul, its smart I feel, its pain is mine.

Nor can the joy you find
In wisdom be denied me or deferred,
In Christ I read each letter and each word.

You cannot flee
From out the bright pale of my prayer,
Nor my swift hand outstretched to touch you anywhere.

If under alien skies
You run from out my song,
The very stones will cry, and prove you wrong.

And should you hide
In the wide deserts of a nameless prayer,
A still, warm presence at your side—I shall be there.

Beneath whatever skies you fly,
Upon what shores you rest,
I am your guest.

Thus read love's covenant—
Engrave it whole
Upon the shining tablets of the soul:

You have no shelter from my love;
Whether you wake or sleep, or dream or die,
Where Christ is, there am I.

THE WAYS OF WISDOM

The ways of wisdom lie beyond our dreaming;
The incidence of love is unforeseen;
How could I take your hand that golden morning
With the tall mountains and the sea between?

But in that country where the soul is native
There are no strangers, nor an alien land;
God turns the summer tides, the winter solstice,
And over seas and years I touch your hand.

The wonder of this word cannot be broken,
Tempered as steel it will outlast the years,
Though for the soul's deep hunger there be silence,
And for its thirst some brimming cup of tears.

Under the ministrations of the spirit
The heart shall grow to freedom sweetly won;
Soul loved by soul is like a towered city
Whose battlements rise glorious in the sun.

Because God set His seal upon your forehead,
And laid a halo on your shining hair,
You light the bright path that we take together
To the last desolate, lonely peaks of prayer.

Because your gates are wide against my coming,
Loosed to my lightest touch each bolt and bar,
My hand within your hand I shall forever
Walk circumspectly as the morning star.

WATER-LILY

You told me of the fragile water-lily
That you had lifted from the garden pool
Where it had cupped the sun and held the starlight
Austere and cool.

I saw your quiet hands above its chalice
Spreading its loveliness against the dark
Where a lone taper tossed its flame, unheeding
That one small spark

Would wake the latent fire in each petal
More than the sun, more than the warmth of spring,
Until its very essence leapt to sudden
New blossoming.

Your vibrant voice upon the empty evening
Fell like a star in water stirred and deep,
Leaving a legacy of gentle wisdom
For me to keep:

This is the symbol of a soul unfettered,
Torn from the pools of pain and held apart,
Lifted in hands made beautiful with blessing,
Schooled at the heart.

This is a soul led swiftly through the midnight
Into the stillness of a holy place
Under the impact of a late tremendous
Summoning of grace.

The heart may feed on a star, a song, a blossom,
But not by these is the reaching spirit stirred
Till there be love, and under its piercing music
The wordless Word!

SUDDEN SONG

How can this song have entered here today
Where through long silences no note has come?
Sweet as the lark that snatched my soul away
Singing above the stones of Tusculum;
Tender as nightingales against the moon;
More sudden than a golden thrush I heard
Above the Ostian gate one summer noon
And wondered were it spirit or a bird.

Only He knows how swift the heart is shaken
Who fashioned it, and mercifully planned
What walls be loosed to sunlight, towers taken
By one soft word, the white strength of a hand;
Only He knows, Who hears the luminous whole
Of music He sets singing in the soul.

NO WIND SHALL BREAK

You tell me that there is no other thing
To hold us close but these keen scimitars
Of shining thought that lift a soaring wing
Like Plato's spirit reaching to the stars;
And then you caution me to guard with care
This new found wonder laid on land and sea,
Lest in the mind's deep winter, unaware
Some brief wind break its subtle potency.

You of the gracious soul, have you not heard
Singing above the whitest thoughts we know,
A voice too intimate for any word,
With warmth to bind the starlight to the snow?
Strong with the strength of God, and wide and deep—
This little secret for your heart to keep.

THERE IS A WISDOM

There is a wisdom nurtured in the soul
Daylight and dark, through sun and blinding snow
The essence of whose bitter, luminous role
We two alone in all the world can know:
Fleet as the dusk is joy upon the heart,
And he who lays his cheek against the bars
That prison loveliness, must dwell apart
And ever walk with sorrow and the stars.

You are so much of beauty that I fear
God made you brief as mist upon the sea;
Yet for this intimate moment you shall hear
The wild, sweet songs that are a part of me—
Songs that will break your heart and make it sing
Till there be music and no other thing.

THIS IS HER DOCTRINE

Love covets no bright trail upon the heights;
She would go fasting in a desert place,
Sleep on the prayer-worn stones the lonely nights
Clothed in the cool austerity of grace;
Her holy converse knows no grill nor bar—
Avila's seraph learned this wisdom well
Who sent her singing by the evening star
To John the mystic kneeling in his cell.
Love knows no terms; there is no bartering
Of word or coin in all her gracious land;
Spendthrift, her heart would spill each shining thing
Into the warm curve of your hesitant hand;
This is her doctrine, and your heritage—
Come, let us kneel and read the luminous page!

SONG IN MY HEART

Now is a moment between birth and death
That I must fill with song; infinity
Trembles upon my lips with every breath
And I must cry for beauty endlessly—
Beauty that lies in small and simple things:
One note that breaks against the heart's warm bars,
Joy on the rim of pain, the light that sings
In silver metaphysics of the stars.

There will be time for silence soft and deep
When springtimes brimmed with blossoms shall go by
Unheeded by the singer who will sleep
With winds and robins under a wide sky—
The tangle of songs in her heart no longer heard
For beauty articulate in one infinite Word.